❦ History *of* Britain ❦
Life in a
Viking
Town

Brenda Williams

Illustrated by John James

HISTORY OF BRITAIN – LIFE IN A VKING TOWN
was produced for Heinemann Children's Reference
by Lionheart Books, London.

Editors: Lionel Bender, Peter MacDonald
Designer: Ben White
Editorial Assistant: Michael Weintraub
Picture Researcher: Jennie Karrach
Media Conversion and Typesetting: Peter MacDonald
Educational Consultant: Jane Shuter
Editorial Advisors: Andrew Farrow, Paul Shuter

Production Controller: Lorraine Warner
Editorial Director: David Riley

First published in Great Britain in 1997 by
Heinemann Educational Publishers, a division of Reed
Educational and Professional Publishing Limited,
Halley Court, Jordan Hill, Oxford OX2 8EJ.

MADRID ATHENS
FLORENCE PRAGUE WARSAW
PORTSMOUTH NH CHICAGO SAO PAULO MEXICO
SINGAPORE TOKYO MELBOURNE AUCKLAND
IBADAN GABORONE JOHANNESBURG KAMPALA NAIROBI

© Reed Educational & Professional Publishing Ltd 1997

ISBN 0 431 05712 5 Hb   ISBN 0 431 05716 8 Pb

British Library Cataloguing-in-Publication Data.
A Catalogue record for this book is available
from the British Library.

Printed in Hong Kong/China

Acknowledgements
All artwork by John James except for map on page 23 by
Stefan Chabluk
Picture credits
t = top, b = bottom, l = left, r = right, c = centre
Pages 4: York Archaeological Trust. 7tr: York Archaeological Trust for
Excavation and Research Ltd. 7cl: C. M. Dixon. 7bl: C. M. Dixon. 8, 9,
10, 11, 12t, 12bl, 15tr, 15bl: York Archaeological Trust. 15lc: C. M.
Dixon. 16b: National Museum of Ireland. 17t: Universitetets
Oldsaksamling, Oslo, Norway. 17b: C. M. Dixon. 18bl: Mick Sharp.
18-19b: Museum of London. 19t: Universitetets Oldsaksamling, Oslo,
Norway. 20, 21: National Museum of Ireland.
Cover: Main illustration by John James. Photos: C. M. Dixon (brooch),
York Archaeological Trust (shoes).

PLACES TO VISIT

Here are some towns, museums and other sites with links to
the Vikings that you can visit. Your local tourist office will be
able to tell you about other places in your area.

British Museum and **Museum of London**, London.
Examples of Viking objects from silver hoards and bronze
brooches to gravestones and bone combs.

Brompton, North Yorkshire. Church with Viking tombstones.

Chester, Cheshire. This important Roman town became a
trade centre for Vikings travelling between Jorvik and
Dublin.

Jorvik Viking Centre, York, Yorkshire. Recreates life in the
Viking town, with reconstructions of houses and finds from
Coppergate and other sites in the most important Viking
town in England.

Lincoln, Lincolnshire. This Roman town was an important
Viking town too. Remains of wooden buildings have been
found at Flaxengate.

Manx Museum, Isle of Man. Viking exhibits. Odd's Cross at
Braddan is a Viking stone carving with runes (inscriptions).

Middleton, North Yorkshire. Stone cross in St Andrew's
Church has a carved figure of a Viking warrior/settler on it.

National Museum of Antiquities, Edinburgh, Scotland. Has
Viking exhibits including objects found in graves.

National Museum of Ireland, Dublin, Ireland. Dublin was the
main Viking settlement in Ireland. The museum has objects
from the Viking town.

Shetland. Early settlements with remains of houses at
Jarlshof, Mainland.

Stamford, LIncolnshire. A Viking town with traces of ditch
defences. A Norman castle was built on the remains of the
Viking fort.

Tullie House Museum, Carlisle, Cumbria. Carlisle had trade
links with the Vikings in Jorvik.

Waterford, southern Ireland. Viking town with later Norman
buildings.

INTRODUCTION

Viking warriors from Scandinavia (Norway, Sweden and Denmark) first made hit-and-run summer raids on the coasts of Britain in AD 789. The Vikings were feared warriors and pirates, but they were also looking for places to settle and build homes.

In 865 several thousand Vikings landed in England and spent the winter in East Anglia. Then part of their army marched north and captured York, which became a Viking town, Jorvik. They ruled Jorvik until 954, when Eric Bloodaxe was driven out by the English king Eadred. The Jorvik Vikings traded with other Vikings in Dublin in Ireland and farther afield. Recent finds in York tell us a lot about the Vikings who lived there, and what they left.

CONTENTS

VIKING JORVIK

When the Vikings captured York in 866, it was a busy trading river-port. York (Jorvik as the Vikings called it) became the most important Viking town in England. Together with Dublin in Ireland, it formed the centre of a united Viking kingdom.

The Vikings captured York from the Northumbrians (who called it Eoforwic). They left it in the hands of 'caretaker' English rulers while they continued fighting the other Saxon kingdoms of Mercia, East Anglia and Wessex. Only Wessex, led by its king Alfred the Great, stayed under Saxon rule.

In 878, Alfred and the Viking leader Guthrum made peace and divided the country. The Vikings were allowed to keep eastern England, from Northumbria to Essex, creating an area later called Danelaw. Viking warriors returned to Jorvik and drove out the English rulers. They took over old buildings which had been set up when York was a Roman fortress-town (Eboracum), and built new farms and workshops. On the banks of the rivers Ouse and Foss they built wharves where ships could land goods. Merchants from Ireland, Scandinavia, Germany and beyond came to Jorvik to trade.

1. River Foss	**5.** Roman army barracks	**9.** King's palace
2. River Ouse	**6.** Bridge	**10.** Coppergate
3. Earl's great hall	**7.** Earth rampart	**11.** Site of Roman bridge
4. Roman wall	**8.** Wooden fence	**12.** Fishergate

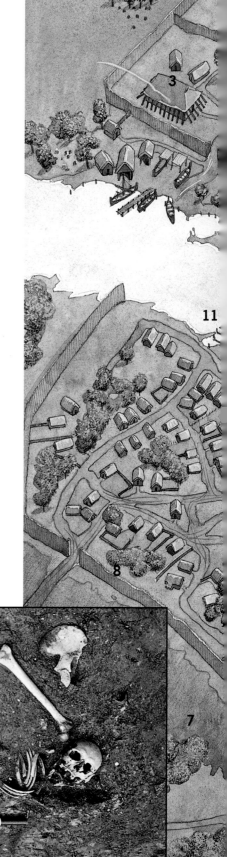

▷ **A 9th-century skeleton found at Coppergate.** This seems to have been a hasty burial, with the body just thrown into a pit. Usually, Vikings were buried with some of their possessions. Maybe this person died in a fight or was a thrall (a poor slave). Finds like this skeleton have revealed fascinating facts about the Vikings in Jorvik.

◁ **A view of Jorvik as if seen from above.** The town developed along the banks of the rivers Ouse and Foss. It grew in size and became a trade centre as the Vikings built harbours and warehouses on the waterfront, along with houses and workshops. The old Roman wall, which still exists, formed a natural defence. The Vikings made new streets, such as Skeldergate (where shield-makers worked). The Viking word 'gata' means street. Coppergate was the street where kopari, or cup-makers, worked.

THE BUSY WATERFRONT

The Vikings were famous for building good ships and making long voyages. An amazing range of goods were brought back to Jorvik's bustling waterfront.

Although many Vikings were farmers, seafaring and trading were also 'in their blood'. Jorvik was not by the sea but it was a port town because the shallow Viking ships could reach it by river. Ships were moored along the river bank, and the waterfront was the heart of the town.

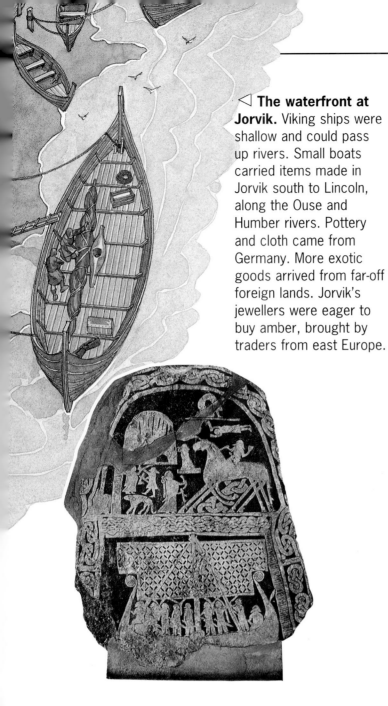

◁ **The waterfront at Jorvik.** Viking ships were shallow and could pass up rivers. Small boats carried items made in Jorvik south to Lincoln, along the Ouse and Humber rivers. Pottery and cloth came from Germany. More exotic goods arrived from far-off foreign lands. Jorvik's jewellers were eager to buy amber, brought by traders from east Europe.

△ **Viking ironwork.** This comes from the door of a church at Stillingfleet near York. It shows part of a Viking ship, with the stern (rear) oar and dragon's head carving. The front of a Viking ship was often carved with a snake's head to look like a sea serpent.

There was much coming and going between Jorvik and Dublin, the main Viking stronghold in Ireland. Merchants from Dublin sailed across the sea and into the Firths of Forth and Clyde, then travelled overland through southern Scotland and across the border into England. Other travellers came from important Viking trading towns in Scandinavia, such as Kaupang in Norway, Birka in Sweden and Hedeby in Denmark (see map on page 23).

Along the waterfront, sailors and merchants unloaded food and wine. Barrels, sacks and bundles were lifted off the ships and taken into storage in warehouses. Materials such as timber, ivory and gemstones were soon being worked in the local craftworkers' shops.

Fragments of silk have been found at Coppergate. Silk was a luxury material, first made in China. It would have begun its journey in Persia, Syria or North Africa, and been bought and sold several times before arriving in Jorvik. By then it was so costly that only a king or his wife could have afforded it.

△ **An 8th-century runestone from Sweden.** Vikings used an alphabet of 16 easy-to-cut letters, or runes, for carving. This stone carving shows Viking gods and a Viking ship.

◁ **A hoard of silver** found in a 10th-century Viking grave. The treasure included Arab coins – evidence of how far the Vikings travelled and traded.

HOUSES AND WORKSHOPS

Archaeologists digging below the streets of modern York have found traces of the houses and workshops of Viking Jorvik. From these finds, we can picture the daily lives of the people of a port town with a new and prosperous activity – making goods for sale.

Stumps of wooden posts that held up the thatched roofs of workshop-homes have been found at Coppergate. Walls were made of woven sticks (wattle), and probably had woollen sheets or animal skins fixed to the inside to keep out the wind and rain. Floors were bare earth, into which were trodden any bits of wood, leather, metal and cloth that fell from the work benches. Food remains and household rubbish were also trodden into the floor.

A Viking leather shoe, found at Coppergate.

△ **Wooden cups** and waste cores from a wood-turner's lathe.

◁ **In Jorvik, people often worked at home.** Some were specialist craftworkers who sold goods to other citizens. But many people did everything themselves – building a new house, mending shoes, making clothes, even killing a cow or a pig for meat.

Jorvik's narrow streets were filled with the sounds and smells of people at work. Carpenters cut wood for building and making simple furniture. Glassmakers sweated over hot kilns. Potters shaped lumps of wet clay into pots and dishes. Tanners prepared leather from animal skins – an especially messy and smelly job. Shoemakers stitched leather shoes.

Over glowing fires, smiths hammered at metal. They made many things of iron, including nails, door hinges, candle holders, spoons, fishhooks, swords and arrowheads. Smiths also worked in tin, lead and copper. Locksmiths made keys and padlocks. Jewellers made pendants, brooches and rings from amber, jet (black fossilized wood), gold and silver. Coins were minted at Jorvik, and the iron dies used for stamping designs on them have been found in the town.

△ **Blacksmiths** made iron tools, weapons and household objects. They heated metal rods and blocks in open fires until they were red-hot. Then they could be bent and shaped using a hammer and anvil.

△ **Pottery** was either roughly shaped by hand or 'thrown' on a potter's wheel. The growing town provided a steady market for Jorvik's potters who began firing storage pots in new and hotter kilns.

△ **Woodworkers** made plates, bowls and cups for everyday use. Such objects were carved by turning wood on a lathe. The woodworkers of Coppergate also made barrels from wooden staves (lengths of wood).

TO MARKET

Trade was an important part of Viking life. Farmers sowed their seeds, then went off on trading journeys until harvest time. They sailed to Scandinavia, to the markets at Birka, Kaupang and Hedeby. Jorvik and Dublin were important markets for foreign traders.

Traders from many lands came to the market at Jorvik, travelling by sea and up the rivers. In places they carried their ships overland. Others rode on horses or walked along the rough tracks that led across mountains and moors and through the thick woods and forests that still covered much of Britain.

The market was the centre of the town's business life. Many of the goods on sale were everyday objects and food, bought and sold cheaply by local people. But there were also rare and expensive luxuries, which only a wealthy ruler or nobleman could afford to buy.

▷ **On market day the streets were crowded.** People brought pigs and sheep to the market to sell. Traders set up stalls in front of the houses, and shouted to attract passers-by. They sold leather belts and shoes, pottery and swords. Everyone was watched over by guards on the defensive wall around the town.

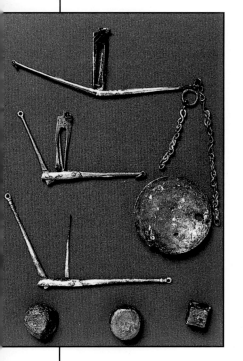

◁ **Folding balance scales**, with pans and lead weights, from Jorvik. Traders carried their own scales to weigh a customer's coins, to make sure they were genuine and work out their value.

Farmers came to town from the countryside, bringing produce to sell. They carried fruit, vegetables, eggs in woven baskets, perhaps a squealing piglet. Hunters came with the furs of wild animals, including wolves (which still roamed parts of Britain). There were seamen from Iceland and Greenland with dried fish and walrus tusks to sell. Merchants brought rare goods from the East, such as strong-smelling spices, costly silk and coins stamped with the likenesses of unknown rulers.

The streets were noisy with the sounds of people exchanging news, arguing over prices, laughing at the latest jokes. Prices were settled by bargaining. People also bartered (exchanged goods). Many merchants carried balance scales, and weighed coins to make sure they were real silver. The people of Jorvik had their own coins, which carried the name of the town's king.

◁ **Some farmers herded sheep to the market** or carried bundles of woollen fleeces to sell to the townsfolk. Others drove flocks of geese, or carried chickens in small cages made of sticks woven together.

△ **A 10th-century die, trial pieces and silver pennies**, found at Coppergate. The die was used to stamp hundreds of coins. A Viking coin did not have a 'face value', like ours. It was valued for its weight. Clipping bits off silver coins made them lighter, and so worth less.

11

THE VIKINGS AT HOME

The Vikings built their homes mainly of wood. The Scandinavian lands they came from were covered with thick forests, so wood was plentiful and the Vikings had become expert carpenters. But most houses in Jorvik were small and, by our standards, not very comfortable.

▽ **A comb and a comb-case** from Jorvik. Combs were usually made from the antlers of red deer.

▽ **Iron keys like these from Jorvik** were used to open padlocks on lids and doors. Viking blacksmiths made the keys by pouring hot molten iron into moulds of different shapes.

Each house in Jorvik was built on its own plot of land. Sometimes the owners dug out a basement, so the floor was below ground level. Wooden posts were driven into the soil to hold up the roof, which was thatched with straw. The upright posts also supported the walls, which were made from wattle – slender sticks of hazel, willow or oak woven in and out of vertical stakes. Each house probably had a front and a back door made of wooden boards with iron hinges. Wooden houses did not last – wood rotted, and fire must have been a frequent hazard, so homes in Jorvik were being repaired or rebuilt all the time.

Inside, a fire in the middle of the floor burned on a hearth made from stones or old Roman tiles. The family slept on wooden beds around the walls, sheltered from damp and draughts by animal skins and woollen fleeces. They had little furniture. They sat on wooden chairs or stools, and a wooden chest used for storing family treasures also served as a table or bench. The house was very dark: it may have had no windows at all. Nor was it very clean. The family may have spread clean straw over the dirt floor, but this would soon have been flattened. As scraps of dropped food and rubbish were trodden in, the floor level rose steadily!

▽ **Houses were built close together.** Each home had a fenced-in plot of land enclosing rubbish and toilet areas. The house could be both a workshop and a home, with the family business carried on at the front. Inside, it was dark, crowded and smoky.

Features of the house
1 Wooden posts
2 Thatched roof
3 Wattle walls
4 Hearth with fire for cooking and warmth
5 Loom for weaving cloth
6 Privy (toilet) behind house
7 Family chest
8 Beds
9 Workshop
10 Hen coop

13

NEW ARRIVALS

In the 11th century there were probably between 10,000 and 15,000 people living and working in Jorvik. Some of these had been born there or in other parts of England. Others had come from overseas. New settlers arrived regularly from Scandinavia. They were seeking a new life in Viking England.

Viking families on the move travelled to new settlements by sea, loading their few possessions on to ships. Passenger ships were slower than the longships used by the warriors. They had a few oarsmen but most of the time they relied on the wind to fill their sails.

When newcomers arrived, their first task was to build a house. Neighbours helped, often eager for news of relatives and friends back home in Scandinavia.

△ **Settlers brought household goods with them in the ship.** A family would own a loom or weaving frame, axes and other tools, buckets and cooking pots. They owned very little furniture apart from the family chest.

△ **New arrivals** from Norway, Orkney and Shetland, or Dublin were used to bitterly cold northern winters. Men wore thick trousers, shirts and sometimes cloaks. Under their long dresses, women wore leggings or socks.

△ **A skilled worker** such as a silversmith hoped to start a good business in Jorvik, selling his goods to the Viking king or a rich merchant. The family brought their tools and other most valued possessions with them.

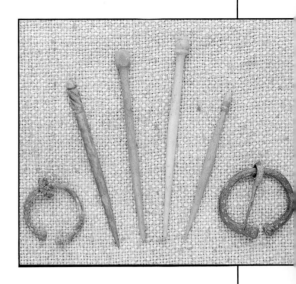

△ **A merchant and his family.** Traders brought back new fashion ideas, such as baggy trousers, from their travels abroad. They also sold slaves. Slaves were made to do dirty work by their owners.

△ **A king and his queen.** Viking kings were warrior-leaders. The more treasure they won in battle, the more warriors they attracted. Settlers coming to live in Jorvik knew they must fight for the king.

△ **Bone hair pins and ring-like brooches** from Jorvik dating from the 900s. The brooches are made of a mixture of copper and other metals. Viking women wore bracelets, rings and brooches.

△ **A Viking metal brooch.**

▽ **Glass beads,** a strap end and a knife handlle found at Jorvik.

Viking settlers in Jorvik came from Scandinavia, Ireland, and other parts of Viking Britain. Some were farmers looking for land. Others were craftworkers, eager to settle in a market town. They felt at home among fellow Vikings, who had the same language, habits and customs.

Among their family treasures, newcomers brought wooden chests, jewels and weapons. Swords were especially valued and were often handed down from father to son. Like all Vikings, newcomers to Jorvik were ready to fight to defend their homes.

Sometimes Jorvik Vikings fought other Vikings as rival kings battled for control of the town and its wealth. They also often fought the English, who in the early 900s were led by the warrior kings Edward and Athelstan. A short-lived truce was arranged, but fighting soon began again.

The townsfolk of Jorvik carried on with their lives amid war and upheaval. Traders still came to Jorvik and the town's market continued to flourish. Newcomers gradually settled in, and their skills added to the busy and bustling life of Jorvik.

A VIKING FEAST

Vikings enjoyed eating and drinking. A feast might last ten days or more. The wedding of a newcomer to a citizen of Jorvik was an occasion for a feast to start the young couple off on their married life. Everyone joined in the party – singing, dancing, drinking and telling stories of the old gods.

In the old religion of the Vikings, there were many gods. The most important were the one-eyed Odin, god of war, and Thor, god of the sky and storms. In Jorvik, many people remembered the old gods, even though now most Vikings in England were Christians. Thor always carried a hammer, and people wore little hammers as lucky charms. Some still made sacrifices to the old gods.

Feasts made a welcome change to the hard work of everyday life. In Jorvik a feast might celebrate a battle, a trading voyage or a birth, as well as a wedding. People also celebrated the start of summer, harvest thanksgiving and midwinter.

▷ **Talk flowed as freely as ale** when Vikings feasted. Men told long, stirring tales, known as sagas. These stories of heroes, gods and monsters were handed down from generation to generation. Sometimes feasting led to loud, hearty singing and to fighting!

▷ **A Viking gaming-board** discovered in Ireland. On the board a type of wargame was played, similar to chess and draughts, by moving pieces between holes. Vikings also liked to play gambling games with dice. Viking children had such toys as wooden weapons and toy boats and would play with these during feasts.

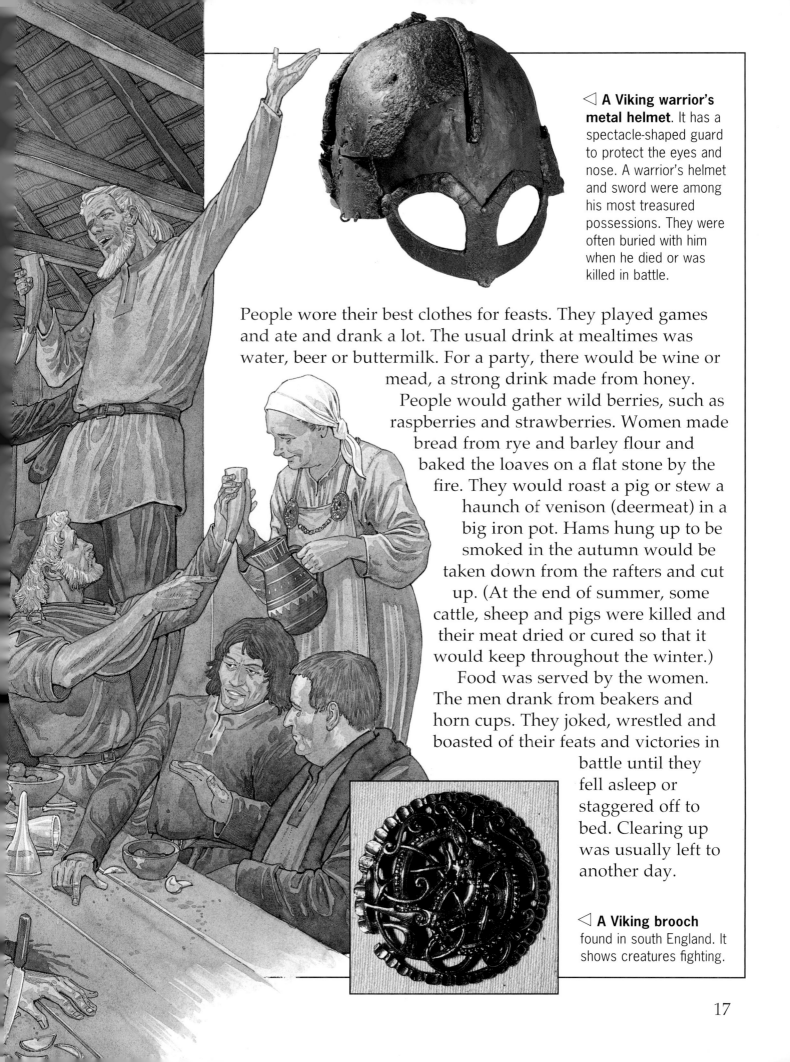

△ **A Viking warrior's metal helmet**. It has a spectacle-shaped guard to protect the eyes and nose. A warrior's helmet and sword were among his most treasured possessions. They were often buried with him when he died or was killed in battle.

People wore their best clothes for feasts. They played games and ate and drank a lot. The usual drink at mealtimes was water, beer or buttermilk. For a party, there would be wine or mead, a strong drink made from honey.

People would gather wild berries, such as raspberries and strawberries. Women made bread from rye and barley flour and baked the loaves on a flat stone by the fire. They would roast a pig or stew a haunch of venison (deermeat) in a big iron pot. Hams hung up to be smoked in the autumn would be taken down from the rafters and cut up. (At the end of summer, some cattle, sheep and pigs were killed and their meat dried or cured so that it would keep throughout the winter.)

Food was served by the women. The men drank from beakers and horn cups. They joked, wrestled and boasted of their feats and victories in battle until they fell asleep or staggered off to bed. Clearing up was usually left to another day.

△ **A Viking brooch** found in south England. It shows creatures fighting.

Ruling and Fighting

The citizens of Jorvik were governed by their king. A Viking king was a warrior-chieftain, who led his soldiers in battle. He also settled disputes. At town meetings, people met to discuss their problems. Jorvik was also a centre for church government, just as York is today.

A warrior king like Olaf Guthfrithsson, who ruled Jorvik from 939 to 941, made war on his neighbours. At his command, men left their homes and went off to fight, hoping to return with plunder. Olaf's Vikings rampaged north into Scotland and south into the English Midlands.

Matters of war and peace were discussed at the town council, called the Thing. This was a kind of parliament which usually met outdoors. In Dublin, townsfolk gathered on a special mound. The king came to meetings to hear complaints, to take advice and to settle quarrels between families. Laws were passed down from one generation to the next. A person who refused to accept the decision of the Thing became an outlaw. His land and goods were taken away and anyone could kill him, without fear of punishment.

The king of Jorvik lived in a 'palace'. It was a large building near the old Roman east gate and a strongpoint in case of attack. The town also had an archbishop. This church leader had his own palace, with a fence around it. Jorvik had a cathedral and several smaller churches made of stones taken from the ruins of Roman buildings.

◁ **Remains of a 9th-century Viking farmhouse** at Jarlshof, Shetland. The homes of Jorvik rulers were similar. The roof was supported by wooden posts and people sat on benches around the walls.

▷ **Axes and spears** used by Vikings in battle.

△ **A Viking chain mail shirt.** Made of small interwoven metal rings, the shirt was worn as protection in battle.

◁ **Warriors return from battle.** They enter Jorvik through the old Roman gate in the wall, repaired by the Vikings. The gate would soon be closed for the night to protect the townsfolk from possible raids. Among the crowd of on-lookers is a child and his mother. They are eager to know if the boy's father is among the warriors safely returned.

Viking soldiers were armed with swords, axes, spears, and bows and arrows. Some rode horses. Remains of Viking saddles, bridles and spurs have been found at Jorvik and in Ireland.

THE END OF JORVIK

From 850 until 954, Vikings in York and Dublin were allies. Their two towns formed a Viking kingdom within the British Isles. Trade flowed between them and Dublin increased its merchant activities after Jorvik's last Viking king was killed.

▽ **An early coin** minted in Dublin in 997, showing King Sihtric Silkbeard, who was defeated by the Irish leader Brian Boru.

▷ **The Viking king and his men arrive at Jorvik from Dublin.** They are welcomed by the town's leaders. Dublin was a base for slave traders, pirates and raiders. Dublin Vikings came regularly to Jorvik. After sailing across the Irish Sea, they sometimes travelled by land over the Pennines, carrying their boats

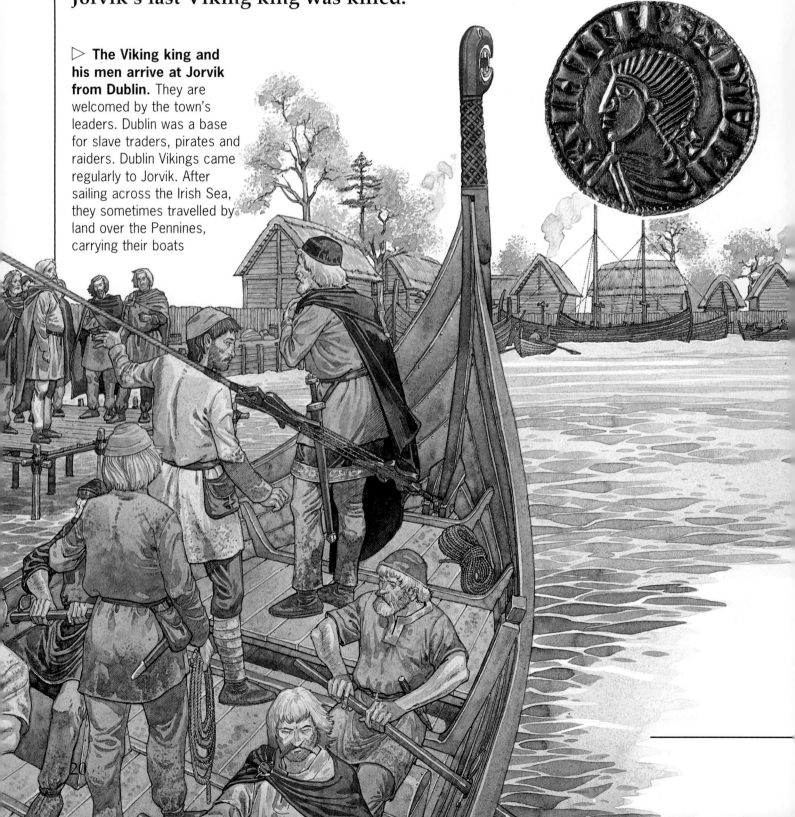

Olaf Guthfrithsson came to Jorvik from Dublin. He was a fierce soldier-king and his attacks showed that the Vikings could still be a threat to their neighbours in Britain. In 947 the Viking leader Eric Bloodaxe, a violent murderer, fled from Norway to Britain. The people of Jorvik accepted him as king, but in 954 he was killed at the Battle of Stainmore.

After Eric Bloodaxe, Jorvik no longer had its own king. The English kings appointed 'jarls' (earls), whom they paid in land to rule the town on their behalf. The earls lived in the Earl's House, near St Olaf's Church.

Jorvik's earls and archbishops were often half-English, half-Scandinavian. The English kings kept a watchful eye on this Viking town in the north. But life for most people in Jorvik went on much as before. They kept their close links across the Irish Sea. In 1014, warriors from Jorvik fought alongside the Dublin Vikings at the Battle of Clontarf, but were defeated by the Irish.

Between 1016 and 1035, the Danish king Cnut united England, Norway and Denmark. This had little effect on Jorvik. Cnut left it alone, and the town held on to what remained of its independence.

▷ **Viking remains in Dublin** were preserved by waterlogged ground. Dublin remained Viking until 1169, when it was overrun by Normans from England.

△ **Weighing coins in the balance.** Trade between Jorvik and Dublin kept many people busy and made both towns rich during the period of Viking rule.

△ **Eric Bloodaxe of Norway** was the last king of Jorvik. He fled to England after killing several of his half-brothers. He met a bloody end in battle.

In 1066 the Jorvik townsfolk aided the Norwegian invader Harold Hardraada. But he was defeated by the English king, Harold II. Then Harold was killed at Hastings. William the Conqueror was king and his Norman soldiers attacked Jorvik. After a fierce battle in 1069, the Normans burned the city and Viking Jorvik was no more. But the city was rebuilt and, as York, it grew and prospered throughout medieval times.

Viking Remains

The Vikings of Jorvik became part of the pattern of British history. Their town vanished, as York grew and changed over the centuries. But they left behind a rich and widespread legacy.

English and Viking families intermarried. The Vikings of Jorvik mingled easily with the English, who spoke a language very like their own. Viking words such as 'sky' and 'knife' passed into English. Place names, such as those ending in -thorpe ('village') or -thwaite ('meadow') are other reminders of our Viking past. The Vikings of Jorvik and Dublin left thriving towns that continue to this day.

▽ **At day's end, the people of Jorvik pack up their goods.** Nightfall brings an end to trading as the town gates are closed. With the coming of the Normans, the Viking way of life also came to an end. During medieval times, Scandinavian Jorvik became English York. Not until the 20th century was Jorvik rediscovered.

GLOSSARY

ale alcoholic drink, like beer.

amber fossilized tree resin, used in jewellery.

archaeology the study of history through the objects left behind by earlier peoples.

archbishop leader in the Church, in charge of an area called a diocese.

craftworkers people with a special skill or trade.

Danelaw land in eastern England under Viking control and ruled by Viking law.

excavation digging for what lies underground.

feud quarrel between members of rival families.

jarl a wealthy chieftain and landowner: 'jarl' became 'earl'.

kiln oven in which clay pots are baked to harden them.

lathe tool used by woodworkers to hold and turn a piece of wood so it can be shaped.

longship Viking warship with oars and one sail.

loom a frame used to weave cloth.

mead an alcoholic drink made from honey and water.

merchants people who made their living by buying and selling, either in their own country or abroad.

pagan person following a religion with many gods and nature spirits.

saga story learned by heart and passed on from person to person.

silk fabric made from fibres spun by silkmoth caterpillars.

smith metalworker making tools, weapons and ornaments of iron and other metals.

Thing Viking council of free men who met to settle disputes.

thrall a slave.

treaty agreement between two sides, for example, to end a war.

wattle building material made from woven sticks.

▽ **Viking Britain.** This map shows the more important places mentioned in this book, including the Places to Visit listed on page 2.

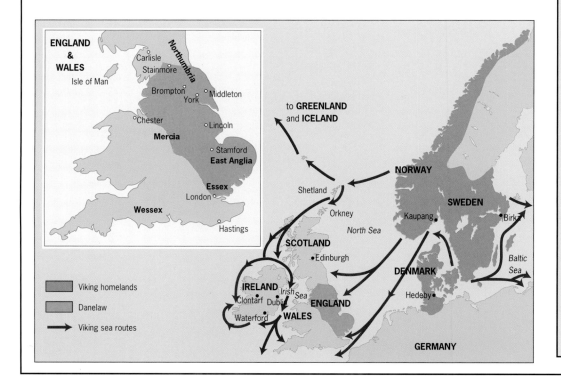

TIMECHART

841 First Viking base in western Europe at Dublin.

865 Great Army of Vikings lands in England.

866 Vikings capture York and rename it Jorvik.

876 Viking soldiers return and remove the English rulers they left in charge of Jorvik.

878 Treaty of Wedmore divides England between Saxons and Vikings.

883 Jorvik has its first known Christian Viking king about this time.

911 Viking leader Rollo becomes the first Duke of Normandy.

917 New settlement at Dublin becomes the main Viking town in Ireland.

919 Raegnald of Dublin makes himself king of Jorvik.

939 Olaf Guthfrithsson is king of Jorvik.

954 Eric Bloodaxe, last Viking king of Jorvik, is killed. Earls rule the town from now on.

999 Irish king Brian Boru captures Dublin.

1014 Irish beat Vikings at Battle of Clontarf.

1066 Viking army of Harold Hardraada beaten in battle by the English.

1066 Norman Conquest of England.

1069 Normans burn Jorvik.

1976 Excavation starts to uncover part of Viking Jorvik, buried beneath the modern city.

INDEX